Soap Making Recipes Book 3: Hot Process Soap Recipes

By

Angela Pierce

Table of Contents

Introduction 5
Soap Making Benefits 6
1. Hot Process Soap Recipe 8
2. HP Soap Sesame Recipe 11
3. Crock Pot Hot Process Soap Recipe 14
4. Swirl Colorful Hot Process Soap Recipe 18
5. Hot Process Soap Avocado Recipe 22
6. Hot Process Rose Scent Soap 25
7. HP Soap Recipe 29
Thank You Page 32

Soap Making Recipes Book 3: Hot Process Soap Recipes

By Angela Pierce

© Copyright 2014 Angela Pierce

Reproduction or translation of any part of this work beyond that permitted by section 107 or 108 of the 1976 United States Copyright Act without permission of the copyright owner is unlawful. Requests for permission or further information should be addressed to the author.

This publication is designed to provide accurate and authoritative information in regard to the subject matter covered. This work is sold with the understanding that the publisher is not engaged in rendering legal, accounting, or other professional services. If legal advice or other expert assistance is required, the services of a competent professional person should be sought.

First Published, 2014

Printed in the United States of America

Introduction

Creativity can't be measured, but it can help man to create innovative solutions for various problems. Whether you are too much or too little creative, it will always help you in your life to do things in a better way and to find enhanced solutions for the problems. Creativity is also consider as a art and when we talk about art it could be anything a painting, a hand craft something or even making soaps. Yes, there are many people who have adopted soap making as their hobby and they are trying new things each day.

With so many brands and types of soaps available in the market, the idea of making soaps at home seems a little bit weird, but the satisfaction and enhancement of creativity while experimenting different colors, pattern and shapes while soap making will make you fall in love with it.

Soap Making Benefits

1. You can create a theme based soaps, occasion based soaps and gift them to your family and friends

2. You can extend your hobby into a business, as to do the things you love will earn you more satisfaction and money.

3. You can customize your own soaps with the fragrance of your choice.

4. You do not need to buy expensive soaps from the market as by adding natural contents you can easily make healthy soaps for yourself.

5. It will help you to properly utilize your free time in something more productive and creative.

6. You do not need to visit grocery stores again and again for buying soaps from the market.

7. You can make your kids learn and it is a great activity to engage with your kids to make their summer a productive and full of learning time.

8. You can give your soaps any shape and design of your choice.

9. Using ingredients also depends on your choice and you can make the soaps healthier for your skin.

Besides these, there are many benefits of soap making at home. There are a variety of ways to adopt for making soaps. Like hot or cold process. You can go for the way you like the most. You can indulge your kids and family in this awesome process of soap making and can enjoy a cheerful and active family time together.

One way to make soap is through hot process. There are many fabulous ways to make hot process soaps, some of the awesome recipes are as follows:

1. Hot Process Soap Recipe

- 12ounces of water

- 1 ounce lavender fragrance oil

- 16 ounces of olive oil

- 16 ounces of coconut oil

- 1 teaspoon of ultramarine

- 4 tbsp. Organic lavender buds (grounded in coffee grinder)

- 4.8 ounces of lye

- 1 ounce of rose petal fragrance

- 0.64 ounce of Shea butter

Instructions:

1. Wipe up the place or sanitize properly everything before start soap making process.

2. Carefully weigh all the ingredients with the exception of lye and put all the things properly on the table.

3. Take the molds and cover them with freezer paper. Now put the cutting board on the stove top and turn on the fan. While dealing with lye you have to be very careful, so always put on your gloves, chemical mask and goggle to keep you safe from any injury from chemical.

PS: never add water to your lye, it could be unsafe for you.

4. Now put the pitcher and measuring scale over cutting board and measure the water in the lye pitcher. Now slowly and gradually add water into it while stirring so that lye must be dissolved completely. Leave the lye on the stove under the fan.

5. Take the crock pot, add in it Shea butter and coconut oil on low heat until they both melt down completely. Now add in it the olive oil and stir the mixture well to mix them all together.

6. Add the water and lye mixture into the oils. Now take the stick blender and stir the both mixtures for 3 minutes until combined well. Now, turn high the crock pot and let the mixture boil for an hour. Do not stir, but keep your eyes on.

7. It will start boiling and folding until you started to see the oil on the top surface. After an hour, stir the mixture, the mixture will look like the mashed potatoes. Add to it all the fragrance oils.

8. Now add in it the coloring and lavender buds. Now put the lid on and let it cook for another 15 minutes.

9. After 15 minutes, stir the mixture well, now check for the lye. Take a bit of the mixture and rub between your hands under running water, if you feel a stinging sensation, then it means you need to cook it again for 20 minutes.

10. Now, after 20 minutes quickly pour it into molds because the hot process soap gets cold and hard quickly and will make it difficult to get them into proper shapes into molds.

11. After pouring the soap mixture into the molds, cover the molds with saran wrapper. With your hands smooth and leveled the soap surface.

12. Now let it cool for 24 hours and then cut it into bars. Let them into a ventilated place to get dried completely for 3 to 4 days. Now you can keep them in a safe place to use when required.

2. HP Soap Sesame Recipe

Hot process soaps are desirable because you do not need to wait for the soap cure time. You can utilize any cold process soap base to make hot process soaps. One thing which you must be careful about in making hot process soap is to carefully handle the lye, which is sodium hydroxide and can cause burns if active. So always have your gloves, goggles and mask on to avoid any injury of burning.

You must have separate equipment for soap making as caustic effect of lye leave it unusable for other things.

Ingredients:

-1 Oz of Shea Butter

- 5 Oz of Coconut Oil

- 3.49 Oz of Lye

- 2 Oz of Sesame Oil

- 9 Oz of water

- 15 Oz of Palm Oil

- ½ teaspoon of Borax (add it in water before adding lye)

- 1 Oz of Castor Oil

Directions:

Take all the ingredients and measure them properly. Keep them in separate bowls or containers. Clean the place where you are intending to prepare the hot process soap.

Put on your gloves to keep yourself safe while dealing with lye and preparing soap. Take the water into a container and add in it lye in chunks and stir well to dissolve all the lye into the water. Carry out it into a well-ventilated environment and never add the water into the lye, always add the lye into a water.

Take all the oils and heat them slowly until they all get mixed together. Now pour the water and lye solution into the oil mixture and stir it well. Carefully mix up the two mixtures until get a little bit hard.

Now cook the mixture on low heat in crock pot for 2 – 3 hours. Keep a close eye on the mixture so that it won't get split out of the pot.

Stir the mixture and if it is glossy and thickened, then check it for lye. Take a bit of mixture on your hand and rub it under running water. If it stings, then it means you need to cook it more for 20 – 30 minutes.

Now mix in it the colorant and fragrance oils. Take the molds and pour the mixture into them. Cover the molds with plastic covering and let it cool for 24 hours. Take out the soap from the bar and place it in a well ventilated spot to get dried further.

As your hot process soap is ready you can store it for future use and even can gift your family and friends. Enjoy the homemade soap with your favorite colors and fragrances.

3. Crock Pot Hot Process Soap Recipe

Ingredients:

- 6.25 Oz of Palm Oil

- Crock pot

- ½ tsp. of yellow oxide

- 1.25 Oz of Meadow Foam Oil

- 1.5 tbsp. of Sunflower Oil

- ½ tsp. of burgundy Oxide

- 1.25 Oz of Shea Butter

- 8.25 Oz of Water

- 2 pound of wood loaf mold (it should be with Wingnuts)

- 8.25 Oz of Olive oil

- 1.40 Oz of Fragrance oil (Sleigh Ride)

- 6.25 Oz of Coconut Oil

- 1.75 Oz of Almond Oil (Sweet)

- ½ tsp. of hydrated chrome green

- 3.50 Oz of Lye (Sodium Hydroxide)

Instructions:

First prepare the coloring, for it you should take half teaspoon of the liquid oil and add in the pigments. Take the electric mixer and mix the coloring in the liquid oil well. Make sure before turning on electric mixture mix the powder pigments little bit to avoid wind up the powder.

In the next step prepare the mold, line in it the freezer paper by keeping the shiny surface above.

Now before moving towards the actual process of the soap preparation, it is recommended to do all safety measures as you are dealing with sodium hydroxide and the hot process soap making involves cooking and heat. For it put on your gloves, goggles and long sleeve shirt to avoid any burning and injury.

Tip: Never add the water into the lye instead always add the lye into the water and stir it slowly to mix it well as lye could be harmful when activated as it could cause burning.

Now first take water in a bowl or container and carefully add lye into it. Stir it slowly until clear and set aside the bowl. Take the coconut and Palm oil, melt them and add Shea butter in it. Add almond, olive oil and meadow foam in it and stir well.

Take the crockpot and pour the oil mixture into it, now slowly add the water and lye mixture into it. Stir them well until a thick mixture is achieved. Put the crock on low and cover it with lid for 15 minutes. After 15 minutes, check the mixture and stir it again for even cooking. The mixture will grow in size and it may come out of the pot, so you have to keep a good eye on it in the first 30 minutes of cooking. Cook the mixture until it seems like mashed potatoes.

The cooking time of the mixture in crock pot depends on the shape and size of the crock. Once your mixture is ready, add in it the Sleigh Ride Fragrance and mix it well. Now divide the mixture into three equal parts and place in separate bowls.

In one bowl, add burgundy oxide, in other yellow oxide and in the last one the hydrated chrome green oxide. Blend well all the three mixtures.

Now take the mold and add the burgundy color mixture at three random places do the same for all the three mixtures until the mold is full. Wrap the mold with plastic cover and even the upper surface of the soap mixture in the mold with your hands to give a smoother look to the soap.

Set aside the mold to dry for 1 – 2 days. Unmold the soap and cut into bars, you can start using the soap right away, but to have the soap last longer in the shower, let it dry in well ventilated environment for at least 4 weeks. Enjoy your colorful hot process soap with heart touching fragrances.

4. Swirl Colorful Hot Process Soap Recipe

Ingredients:

-1 Teaspoon of titanium dioxide

- 7.5 Oz of Palm Oil

- 2 pound wood mold (loaf)

- 1.5 Oz of Mango Fragrance Oil

- 7.5 Oz of Olive Oil

- ½ teaspoon of electric bubble gum pigment

- 2.5 Oz of Sunflower Oil

- 7.5 Oz of Coconut Oil

- 3.4 Oz of Lye

- ½ Teaspoon of Merlot mica

- 8.25 Oz of Water (Distilled)

- 1 Teaspoon of hydrated green chrome oxide

- 2.5 Oz of Sweet Almond Oil

Directions:

Take the wooden mold and line it with freezer paper by keeping the shiny surface facing upward. For safety purpose put on your gloves, goggles and full sleeve clothes to avoid any injury or burning as we are dealing with lye (sodium hydroxide) which could be injurious when active).

First of all we prepare the colorings for it, take 1 tablespoon of liquid oil and ass in it titanium dioxide, take ½ teaspoon of electric bubble gum and add in ½ tbsp. of liquid oil and finally, take 1 tbsp. of liquid oil and add in it 1 teaspoon of chrome green oxide. Mix them well with electric mixer.

Tip: To avoid wind up make sure to mix the powder little bit in the liquid before turning on the electric mixer.

Now take the distilled water and carefully add in it the sodium hydroxide, stir till clear and keep it aside. Take the oils and melt them on low heat in crock pot, mix them well. Pour into oil mixture the water and lye solution slowly and stir the both mixtures well until a thick mixture has formed.

Now divide the mixture into three and add in each the different coloring pigment. In one of the mixture, add 1 teaspoon of dispersed electric bubble gum pigment and ½ teaspoon of Merlot mica. In second mixture, add 3 teaspoon of titanium dioxide and in third mixture portion add 2 teaspoons of hydrated chrome green oxide. Mix the colorants well in the mixture.

In each mixture, add 0.5 Oz of Mango fragrance oil and stir it well. Now take the mold and start pouring the three mixture like that, pour the Red soap mixture in the middle, white in the sides and Green on the place left. Repeat again the layering process by again pouring the Red over the green, white and then green again until the mold is full.

Tip: Let one layer penetrate into another to clear the better swirling effect.

Using a chopstick or any other stick, create the swirls by moving it first perpendicular and then horizontal along the mold.

Turn on the oven and preheat it to 170 degrees, now place the mold into the oven and let it cook for 1 hour. After 1 hour, turn off the oven and replace the mold from it. Leave it to cool down for overnight or for 24 hours. Unmold the soap and cut it into fine bars of medium size, you can see a beautiful swirling effect on the soap. Place the soap bars in well ventilated place to get dry for 3 – 4 weeks. Although you can use it right away, but if you wish your soap to last longer, then it's better to give it a good cure time to enjoy your favorite color and scented soap for long.

This beautifully swirl and colored soap is perfect for Christmas gift to your loved ones and you can even use the fragrance of your choice to enjoy the refreshing bath.

5. Hot Process Soap Avocado Recipe

Ingredients:

- 435 grams of Coconut Oil

- 136 grams of Safflower oil

- 312 Grams of Avocado Oil

- 517 grams of water - 136 grams of Shea butter

- 204 grams of almond oil

- 193 grams of Lye

- 136 grams of Mango butter

Instructions:

Clean the area where you are intending to prepare the soap. Take on your gloves and full sleeve clothes to protect yourself from any injury. Make sure your kids and pet won't disturb you in between the process. So choose the time when you are completely free of your other responsibilities, as hot process soap required careful look during the whole procedure.

Well, after that weight all the oils and mix them all. Take a crock pot on low and let the oils melt down in the pot. Take the water and add in it the lye, make sure to carefully add the lye into water and stir slowly until it's clear and now mix it into the oils in the crock pot. Mix them well until a thick mixture formed, you can use a wooden stick to mix them together.

Now set the crock pot on low heat and cove it with lid. Let it cook for an hour. Check in between and stir to make sure the mixture cook evenly. Cook till mixture will look like mash potatoes and get thick.

Now it is ready to go into molds, but before that add in it the fragrance oil or colorants of your choice. If you are using any fragrance or colorants then start with adding colorants and additive first. Mix them well with the mixture. Do not add fragrance first as mixture is too hot. Let it little bit cool and add in it the fragrance oil. Mix the oil with the mixture with the wooden spoon.

Take the mold of your choice, it could be of any shape and size. You can also choose some design molds available in the market. Carefully line up the mold with the freezer paper. Now pour the mixture into the mold until the mold gets filled completely.

Do not touch the mixture directly, as it can burn your hands. Wrap the mold with the plastic cover and using your hands level the upper surface of the mixture to give it an even look.

Keep the mold for 24 hours to cool down. Once done unmold the soap and cut it into different shapes or bars. You can use your soap right away, but if you want to have them longer in shower then it is good to let them dry out completely for 3 – 4 weeks. This way the soap will get hardened well and last longer.

You can give these soaps as a gift to your family or friends and can even open a homemade soap business. Even for your own self you can prepare the soaps of your favorite fragrance and color at home with this quick hot process soap recipe.

6. Hot Process Rose Scent Soap

If you love rose fragrance, then it's a perfect soap for you to try at home with simple ingredients and less cooking time.

Ingredients:

- 12 Oz of water (Distilled)

- 16 Oz of Olive oil

- 1 Oz of Rose Fragrance oil

- 0.64 Oz of Shea butter

- I tbsp. of ultramarine purple

- 4 tbsp. of organic lavender buds

- 16 Oz of Coconut oil

- 1 Oz of Lavender Fragrance Oil

- 4.80 Oz of lye

Instructions to prepare:

Make sure to sanitize everything like mold, containers and things you are going to use for soap making to ensure healthy and safe soaps for your family.

Take all the ingredients and weight them carefully. Take the mold and lined it up with the freezer paper having shiny side upward.

Put on your gloves and goggles as you are dealing with lye, which if used carelessly can cause any injury. So after Cleaning safety comes first. Now take the water in a container or a bowl and add in it bit by bit the lye. Be more cautious and never ever add water into the lye, always remember to add lye into water. Stir till color get clear and set the container aside.

Now take all the oils like olive oil, coconut oil and Shea butter and pour into crock pot set at low. Let them let completely and mixed well. Now slowly and carefully pour into the solution of water and lye into it. Stir the mixture until combined.

Now put the crock pot on low and cover it with the lid to cook for an hour or two. Keep checking on the mixture in between by stirring and watching after sometime. Do not worry if you see the mixture get increased in quantity. Let it cook until the mixture look like the mashed potatoes.

Now your mixture is ready for further processing. Turn off the heat and let it little bit cool, almost 10 – 20 degrees low. Now add in the fragrance oils and mix it well with the mixture until combined together. You can also add color and pigments if you want otherwise it is good to go for cooking another 15 minutes.

After 15 minutes, stir the mixture well and check if it is ready to go in the mold or not. Do this simple test, take a little bit of mixture on hand and rub between your hands under water. If it stings then you need to cook it again for 20 minutes.

Do not let the soap cool down before pouring into the molds as it gets hard too quickly. So carefully pour into the mold and wrap it with saran wrapper. As the surface of mixture look uneven to even it use your hands and level the surface of the mixture in the mold.

Your soap is ready to go on cooling mode for 24 hours. After 24 hours unmold the soap and cut it according to your need or cut it into bars. If you want to use the soap for longer, then it is better to let them dry out for 3 -4 weeks to get hardened enough to survive in the water for longer. So your rose fragrance soap is ready to refresh your bath time with its pleasant scent and keep you active and lively for long. Enjoy this recipe and make healthy soaps for your family.

7. HP Soap Recipe

Ingredients:

-14.2 Oz of Palm Oil

- 20 Oz of water

- 9.2 Oz of Lye

- 30.8 Oz of Olive oil

- 2.5 Oz of Fragrance Oil

- 18.9 Oz of Coconut Oil

Instructions:

First of all make sure that you have put on your goggles and gloves and also a long sleeve shirt. It is for safety measure and good to protect yourself from any harm. Next it is necessary to have everything cleaned and clear to prepare healthy and germ free soaps for your family.

Weight out all the ingredients properly and place it carefully at one place to start making the soap easily and without any hide and seek. Also keep the children and pet away from the room you are using to prepare the soap. Make sure the room is well ventilated to avoid the fumes.

Take the water and add in it the lye, stir it well until the solution gets clear. Next take the olive, coconut and palm oil in the crock pot on low to melt them down completely. Now add in the lye and water solution slowly and stir it well until get mixture is formed.

Now put the crock on low and cover it with the lid to cook for 1- 2 hours. Do not go away, as it is necessary to keep an eye on the mixture while it's cooking. Stir it after some time in between cooking to ensure even cooking of the mixture.

First it will convert into a gel and then looks like a mash potatoes. Stir the mixture well and test it for lye by taking a little bit of it and rub on your hands under water. If it stings your hands then you need to cook it again for 1 minutes.

After that, turn off the heat and wait for the mixture to cool down a bit and add in it the fragrance. At this point you can also add in it any colorant or additive of your choice. Now take the mold lined it up with the freezer paper and pour in it the soap mixture. Wrap the mold with the saran paper. Even the surface of the mixture by pressing with your hands. Let the mixture cool down for 24 hours.

Unmold the soap and cut it down into soap bars. For better dry soaps it is good to keep them to dry out for 3 – 4 weeks.

The hot process soaps can be easily made at home and more economical than other soaps in the market. The best thing is you can not only enjoy the creative time while making soap at home but also can customize the shape, color and fragrance of the soap according to your choice or your loved ones and can prepare the best Christmas and Easter gift for your family.

Thank You Page

I want to personally thank you for reading my book. I hope you found information in this book useful and I would be very grateful if you could leave your honest review about this book. I certainly want to thank you in advance for doing this.

www.ingramcontent.com/pod-product-compliance
Lightning Source LLC
LaVergne TN
LVHW021946060526
838200LV00042B/1932